DATE DUE

DESIGN AND CREATE

Wheels and Cars

John Williams

RSVP

RAINTREE
STECK-VAUGHN
P U B L I S H E R S
The Steck-Vaughn Company

Austin, Texas

Published by Raintree Steck-Vaughn Publishers, an imprint of Steck-Vaughn Company

Library of Congress Cataloging-in-Publication Data
Williams, John.
Wheels and Cars / John Williams.
    p.   cm.—(Design and create)
    Includes bibliographical references and index.
    Summary: Provides step-by-step instructions for making different kinds of vehicles which require wheels.
    ISBN 0-8172-4887-0
    1. Toy making—Juvenile literature.
    2. Vehicles—Models—Juvenile literature.
    [1.Toy making. 2. Vehicles—Models.
    3. Models and modelmaking.]
    I. Title. II. Series: Williams, John, 1939- Design and create.
    TT174.5.V43W55   1998
    745.5—dc21   96-1262

Printed in Italy. Bound in the United States.
1 2 3 4 5 6 7 8 9 0 02 01 00 99 98

Commissioned photography by Zul Mukhida

CONTENTS

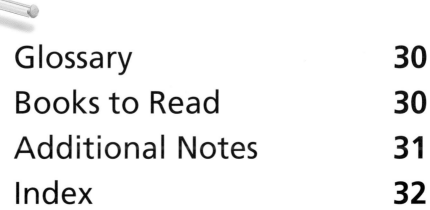

INTRODUCTION

From bicycles to jumbo jets, almost every type of transportation uses wheels. Wheels let people move heavy loads over land. Although a load can be dragged along the ground, putting wheels underneath makes moving it much easier.

To move big things before wheels were invented, people put round poles underneath them. The large stones used to build the pyramids in Egypt, and Stonehenge in England, were probably rolled along in this way.

The first wheels were made of solid wood. Later, spokes were invented, and metal took the place of wood. Rubber tires were used as long ago as 1845, but they did not work well at first.

Vehicles need to be designed for the types of loads that they have to carry. The designs for a garden wheelbarrow or a school bus are very different, but each one is ideal for the job it has to do.

There are many different types of vehicles that have wheels. Some are pulled by animals such as horses or by people. Others have gasoline engines, but engines can also work with electricity and even natural gas. Not all vehicles have four wheels. How many different types can you see in this street in India?

A monorail is a type of electric train. Instead of running on two tracks with wheels on either side, it runs on one central track. Some monorails do not need engineers. Instead, they are totally controlled by a computer.

For hundreds of years, all vehicles were made mainly of wood and were pulled by horses. When steam and gasoline engines were developed, the designs of vehicles began to change.

Technology has helped to make modern vehicles safer and more comfortable. However, more and more people own cars, and trucks are becoming larger all the time. The fumes and noise from their engines can cause pollution. People who design and make these vehicles will have to solve these problems in the future.

Most modern bicycles now have light frames and many gears. But the basic design of the bicycle has changed very little since it was first given two equal-sized wheels.

WOBBLY WHEELS

What happens when wheels are not round? Here is a simple cart to make with oval wheels.

Wheels are usually attached to rods or tubes, called axles. Axles are made of wood or metal. They can be very short with just one wheel on them, such as at the front of a wheelbarrow or a tricycle. Other axles are longer, and have a wheel at each end.

YOU WILL NEED

- A shallow box or box lid

- Two pieces of .25 in.-(5mm-) diameter dowel, .5 in. (1cm) longer than the width of the box

- Four round wheels made from heavy cardboard, with .25 in. (5mm) center holes

- Hole punch

- Hobby knife or coping saw

- Glue and scissors

- Pencil and ruler

- Plank of wood

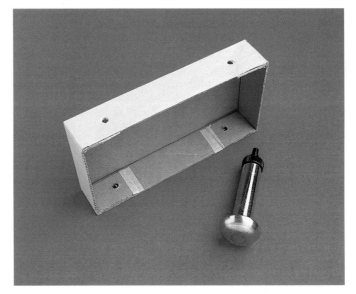

1 Punch two holes in the sides of one end of the box. They should be exactly opposite each other. Punch two more holes at the other end.

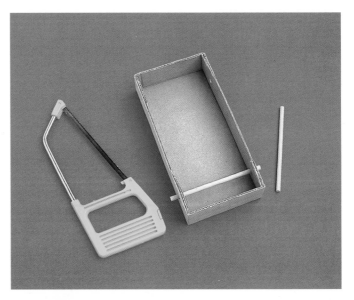

2 Cut the dowel so that each piece is just .5 in. (1 cm) longer than the width of the box. Slide the dowels through the holes. They should turn easily.

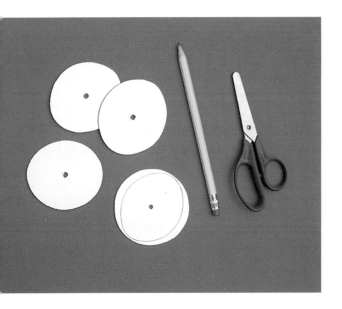

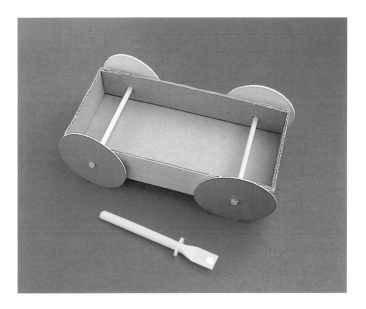

3 Draw an oval on one of the round wheels. Cut out the oval shape. Use this as a emplate to make each wheel the same size nd shape.

4 Push a wheel onto each end of the dowels. Make sure each pair is pointing the same way. Put a little glue on each wheel to attach it to the axle.

5 Make a steep slope with a plank of wood. Run your cart down the slope. What happens with the oval wheels?

NOW TRY THIS

Change the oval wheels for different-sized pairs of round wheels. Keep the small wheels on one side and large wheels on the other. What happens?

7

HOVERCRAFT

A hovercraft is one of the few forms of land transportation that does not need wheels. Instead, it is held up by a powerful jet of air that is pushed downward, against the land or the sea. This cushion of air allows the hovercraft to move easily in any direction.

Hovercraft are used to travel across water. This large one can transport many cars and hundreds of people.

YOU WILL NEED

● Thin Styrofoam at least 8 in. (20 cm) square

● Short cardboard tube, about 1 in. (3 cm) in diameter

● Tissue paper

● Glue

● Steel ruler

● Hobby knife & scissors

● Pencil

● Hair dryer (optional)

1 Mark a square of about 6 in. or 8 in. (15 cm to 20 cm) on the Styrofoam. Carefully cut out the square using the hobby knife and a steel ruler.

2 Hold the cardboard tube in the center of the Styrofoam and draw around it. Ask an adult to cut a round hole, using the hobby knife. Put a little glue on the end of the tube and push it into the Styrofoam. Let the glue dry.

3 Cut a long piece of tissue paper for the hovercraft's skirt. It should be about 1 in. (2 cm) longer than the distance around the Styrofoam, and be about 1.5 in. (4 cm) wide.

4 Glue the paper skirt all the way around the side edge of the Styrofoam. Where the ends meet, let them overlap and glue them together. Let the glue dry.

5 Blow down the tube or use a hair dryer to make a current of air. What happens to the Styrofoam square?

NOW TRY THIS

Try changing the design of the hovercraft. Make the Styrofoam square bigger or smaller, and the skirt longer or shorter. What size works best?

ROMAN CHARIOT

YOU WILL NEED

- Corrugated plastic, .25 in. (5 mm) thick

- Wooden dowel, .25 in. (5 mm) diameter

- Two wooden wheels, about 2 in. (5 cm) in diameter, .25 in. (5 mm) thick, with .25 in. (5 mm) center holes

- Two cardboard circles, about 1 in. (2.5 cm) in diameter, with .25 in. (5 mm) center holes

- Small pieces of PVC tubing, about .25 in. (5 mm) in diameter and .25 in. (5 mm) long

- Metal paper fasteners

- Cardboard, felt, string, pipe cleaners, tissue paper

- Rubber bands

- Masking tape

- Small hacksaw

- Pencil, ruler, & scissors

The ancient Romans lived before cars, trains, or even bicycles were invented. They used horses to pull chariots that carried one or two people. Because the chariots were small and light, they could move quite quickly.

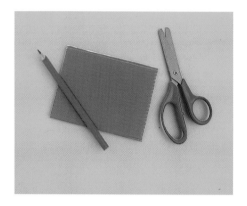

1 Cut a rectangle out of corrugated plastic, about 4 in. x 3 in. (10 cm x 8 cm), with the lines in the plastic running in the same direction as the long sides.

2 Cut a piece of dowel about .75 in. (2 cm) longer than the long side. Push it through the plastic in the center to make a fixed axle.

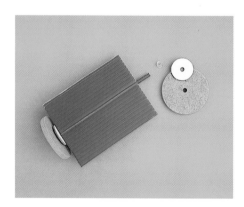

3 Put the wheels on each end of the dowel. Add the small cardboard circles first, then the wooden wheels. Slip the PVC tubing over the end of the dowel to hold the wheels.

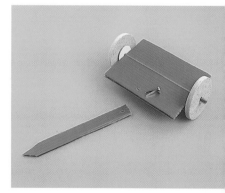

4 Cut a long, narrow piece of plastic to make the pulling shaft. It should be about 5.5 in. (14 cm) long. Join it to the rectangle, in the middle, with a metal paper fastener.

5 Cut out a narrow piece of plastic to go around three sides of the rectangle. Bend it where it will go around the corners. Join it to the rectangle with masking tape.

Roman chariots could go quite fast. They did not weigh very much and usually carried only one or two people. Besides using them to get from one place to another, the Romans held chariot races. This is a modern chariot, made in the same way as the Roman ones.

6 Make two model horses to look as though they are pulling the chariot. Try using cardboard, felt, string, pipe cleaners, and tissue paper. Also make some "animal skins" to line the chariot.

JET-POWERED CAR

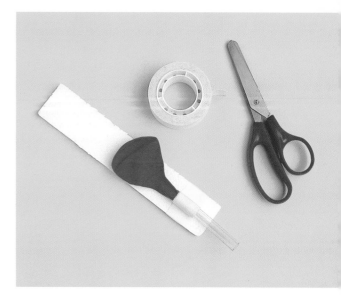

1 Cut the lip from the balloon. Put the plastic tube into the mouth of the balloon. Pull the end tightly around the tube and attach it with masking tape. Make sure no air can escape.

2 Using the hobby knife and steel ruler, cut a piece of Styrofoam about 6.5 in. (16 cm) long and 1.5 in. (3 cm) wide. Attach the balloon with masking tape so that the tube is at one end

YOU WILL NEED

- Styrofoam .5 in. (1.5 cm) thick
- Balloon
- Flexible PVC tubing, about 2.5 in. (6 cm) long
- Pushpins
- Cardboard
- Masking tape
- Hobby knife
- Steel ruler
- Pencil
- Scissors

Jet engines are sometimes used for special racing cars. They give a strong, hard push so the car will go very fast. The air from a balloon will move a model car, but the car must be very light and simple.

A hobby knife can be dangerous if it is not used properly. Always ask an adult to help you use one.

- **Always use a steel ruler to guide the knife.**

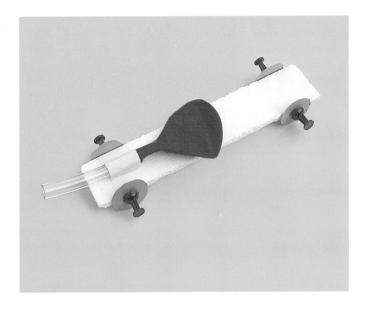

3 Cut out four cardboard wheels about .75 in. (2 cm) in diameter. Put a pushpin through the center of each wheel. Make sure that the wheels can move freely on the pins.

4 Push the pins into the sides of the Styrofoam, 1 in. (2 cm) from each end. Leave just enough of the pins sticking out for the wheels to turn freely.

A jet ski has an engine that pushes out strong jets of water. They make the ski move very fast over water, but the ground is too hard and bumpy for them to work on land.

5 Blow up the balloon. Keep your finger over the mouth of the tube. Put the buggy on a very smooth surface and let go.

NOW TRY THIS

Design an even smaller car. Will a bigger balloon make any difference?

MOON BUGGY

When astronauts landed on the moon in the 1970s, they took with them some special vehicles. Obviously, there are no roads on the moon. One of the main problems with driving there were the many loose rocks, so their electric buggies were built with large knobby wheels to grip the ground.

YOU WILL NEED

- Heavy cardboard

- Two plastic drinking straws, about .25 in. (6 mm) in diameter

- Wooden dowel, less than .25 in. (5 mm) in diameter

- 8 circles of thick cardboard for wheels, about 2.5 in. (6 cm) in diameter, with center holes to match the dowel

- Corrugated cardboard to go around the wheels

- Masking tape

- Glue

- Hole punch

- Pencil

- Ruler

- Scissors

- Small hacksaw

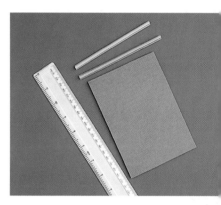

1 Cut a rectangle of heavy cardboard to form the base of the buggy. One measuremen should be about the same lengt as the straws.

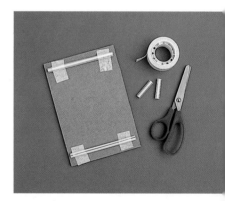

2 Tape a straw near each shorter end of the cardboard. The straws should be about .5 in. (1 cm) in from the edge of the cardboard and exactly parallel to the edge.

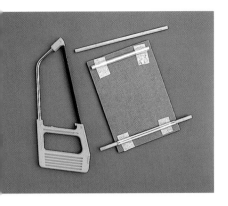

3 Cut two lengths of dowel for the axles. They should be 2 in. (5 cm) longer than the short side of the cardboard rectangle. Push the dowel through the straws. The axles should be able to move freely.

4 Cut four strips of corrugated cardboard 1 in. (2 cm) wide and long enough to fit around the edges of the wheels. Glue the edges of each piece of cardboard to a pair of disks to make four wide wheels.

5 Push the wheels onto each end of the dowels. Attach the wheels to the dowels with a little glue.

NOW TRY THIS

You will have to design what to put on the top of this chassis. Make some drawings showing special seats for the astronauts, radio antennas, and even a flag. Make these out of cardboard and attach them to the chassis.

The moon vehicles were called lunar rovers. They let the astronauts explore much farther from the landing sites than was possible on earlier missions. The cars had to be left behind; they are still on the moon.

CABLE CAR

YOU WILL NEED

- Two small blocks of wood
- Two cup hooks
- Two C-clamps
- Rubber bands
- Heavy fishing line
- Three small boxes
- Paper clips
- Two thread spools
- Thin wire or pipe cleaners and wire cutters
- Cardboard
- Weight, such as modeling clay, or small toy
- Glue
- Masking tape
- String or heavy thread
- Scissors

This type of transportation does not have wheels that move along the ground. It hangs from thick wires and is pulled by cables or ropes. A cable car uses special wheels called pulleys, over which the cables or ropes have to move. The pulleys may be attached to the car or at each end of the cable.

Cable cars are often used to take people up to the tops of mountains. On the way, the passengers have a wonderful view of the mountain scenery. This cable car is in Switzerland. It can carry more than 40 people at one time.

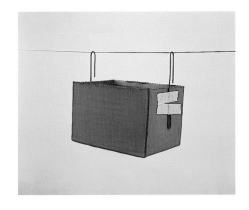

You need to attach the ends of the cable firmly. Screw the up hooks into two small blocks f wood. Fix the blocks tightly o two tables with C-clamps. Ask n adult to help you.

2 Cut a piece of fishing line. Tie a rubber band to each end of the line. Put one rubber band over each of the cup hooks so that the bands stretch and keep the line taut.

3 Straighten out two paper clips, leaving one bend at each end. Use masking tape to attach the clips to opposite ends of a box. Use the hooked ends to hang the box on the line.

NOW TRY THIS

- **See how much load you can carry in the cable car.**
- **Send messages from one end of the room to the other.**
- **Can you design and make a cable car that goes uphill?**

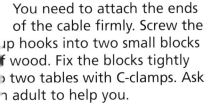

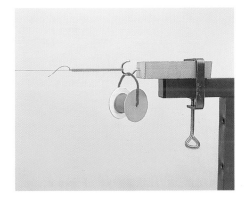

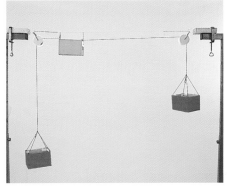

4 Cut four circles of cardboard, a little wider than the ends of the thread spools. Glue the circles on each end of the spools and let the glue dry. Cut two pieces of wire or take two pipe cleaners. Use them to hang the cotton spools from the cup hooks.

5 Use masking tape to attach some thread to each end of the box. Pass the ends over the spools. Attach the free ends of the threads to the other boxes so that they hang below the spools. Make sure that there is enough thread to pull the cable car the complete length of the fishing line.

6 Put a weight in one box so that as it falls it pulls the cable car along. The box at the other end will lift up. Exchange the weights to bring the cable car back.

TRAIN CAR AND TRACKS

Trains and streetcars, which run on rails, have to have special wheels with metal lips, called flanges. These keep the train on the rails. The flanges go on the insides of the rails.

YOU WILL NEED

- Small cardboard box

- Two pieces of .25 in. (5 mm) dowel, 1 in. (2 cm) longer than the width of the box

- Four round wheels made from cardboard, about 1.5 in. (4 cm) in diameter, with center holes to match the dowel

- Four wooden wheels, about 1 in. (3 cm) in diameter, .25 in. (5 mm) thick, with center holes to match the dowel

- Wood, about .5 in. (1 x 1 cm) square: two long lengths

- Poster board (for roof)

- Hole punch

- Glue

- Pencil, ruler, & scissors

- Paint and paintbrush

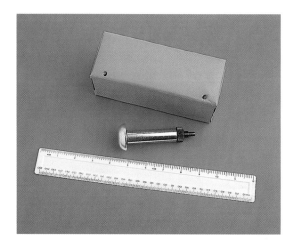

1 Punch four holes in the sides of the box, about .75 in. (2 cm) from each end. Make sure that they are exactly opposite each other and about .5 in. (1 cm) from the bottom of the box.

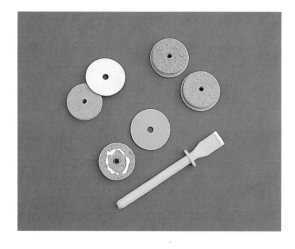

2 Glue one thick wooden wheel onto each of the larger cardboard wheels. Make sure the holes in the center overlap exactly. The cardboard wheel will form the flange.

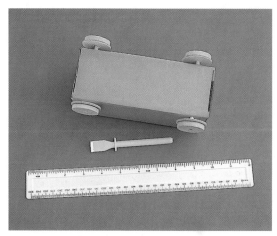

3 Push the dowel axles through the holes in the box. Glue a wheel onto each end so that the flange is on the inside. Make sure the wheels are straight. Each pair must be the same distance apart.

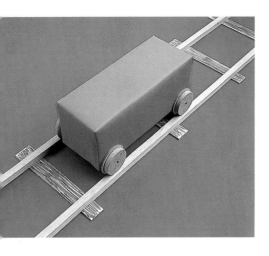

4 Use long lengths of the .5 in. wood for the rails. Stick them to pieces of cardboard. They should be the same distance apart as the wheels.

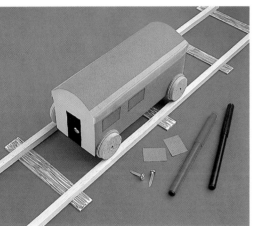

5 Decorate the train car and add the windows and doors. Make a roof with a curved piece of poster board.

NOW TRY THIS

Put a small electric motor (1.5V–4.5V) in the center of one end of the tracks. Wire it to a battery (4.5V minimum). Glue a piece of heavy thread to the front of the train car. Tie the other end of the thread to the spindle of the electric motor. The motor will pull the car along the track.

Most modern trains get their power from electricity or sometimes from diesel fuel. This is an older steam engine in China.

CARRIAGE WITH SUSPENSION

YOU WILL NEED

- Small cardboard box, about 4 in. x 5.5 in. (10 x 14 cm)

- Wood, about .5 in. (1 cm) square

- Two cardboard triangles, each side about 1.25 in. (3 cm) long

- Four round wheels made from cardboard, about 2 in. (5 cm) in diameter

- Four pushpins

- Thin wire, such as plastic-covered florist's wire

- Masking tape

- Glue

- Small hacksaw

- Pencil

- Ruler

- Scissors

- Paints and paintbrush

There are many different kinds of spring mechanisms on modern vehicles. They are all designed to protect the vehicle and its passengers from damage when they are traveling over rough ground. Modern suspension systems can be a complicated collection of springs and levers, but many years ago a flexible piece of metal or even wood was all that was used.

Carriages pulled by horses carried freight and passengers. This is an artist's picture of a mail coach, nearly 200 years ago. The man at the back is throwing down a mailbag to the person on the ground. The passengers traveled inside as well as on top of the carriage.

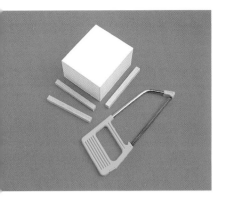

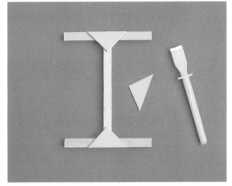

1 Cut two pieces of wood a little wider than the box. Cut one piece the same length as the box.

2 Put a little glue on each end of the long piece of wood, and join it to the center of each of the short pieces. For added strength, glue on the two cardboard triangles over each join.

3 Cut four short lengths of the garden wire. Make a small loop in one end of each piece. Bend each piece into a C shape with the loop at right angles to the C.

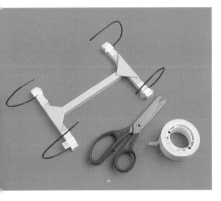

4 Using masking tape, attach each piece of wire to the wooden frame. The looped end of the wire should be stuck flat to the wood, about .25 in. (5 mm) in from the wheel. Stick the other ends of the wire to the underside of the box.

5 Join the wheels to the frame with pushpins. Put a pin through the center of each wheel. Make sure each wheel can turn freely.

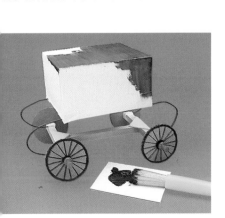

6 Decorate your box to look like an old horse-drawn carriage. It should have windows and doors on each side.

TRAILER WITH STEERING HANDLE

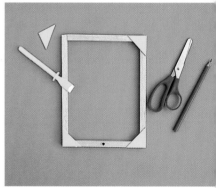

Vehicles need ways of steering, to help them go around corners. The front wheels of modern cars and trucks can move to the left or to the right, but with old-fashioned carts and trailers it was often just the shafts and handles that turned.

YOU WILL NEED

- Wood, about .5 in (1 cm) square: two pieces 7 in. (18 cm) long, three pieces 5 in. (12 cm) long

- Wooden dowel, .25 in. (5 mm) in diameter: two pieces 6.75 in. (17 cm) long

- Wooden dowel, .25 in. (5 mm) in diameter: two pieces 1.5 in. (3 cm) long (for handle)

- Small piece of cardboard

- Four circles of heavy cardboard for wheels, about 1.5 in. (4 cm) in diameter, with center holes to match the dowel

- Glue

- Hand drill with .25 in. (5 mm) drill bit

- Needle file (optional)

- Hole punch

- Pencil

- Ruler

- Scissors

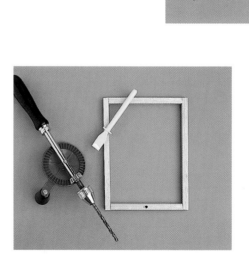

1 Drill a hole through the center of a 5 in. (12 cm) length of wood. This piece will be the front part of the chassis. Glue this piece, another 5 in. (12 cm) length, and the two 7 in. (18 cm) lengths together to make a frame.

2 Lay the frame flat on the table. Cut four triangles of cardboard with two sides 1.5 in (3 cm) long and a base 2 in. (4.5 cm) long. Glue the triangle to each corner of the wooden frame, as in the picture.

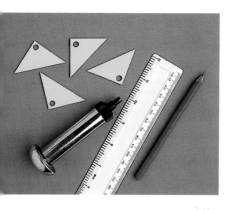

3 Cut four more triangles with two sides about 1.5 in. (4 cm) long and a longest side of 2 in. (5 cm). Punch holes near the points made by the shorter sides. Make sure they are all in the same place on each triangle.

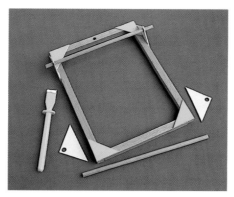

4 Attach the triangles to the sides at each end of the long pieces of wood. Make sure each pair of triangles is exactly opposite each other, and pass the long pieces of dowel through the holes.

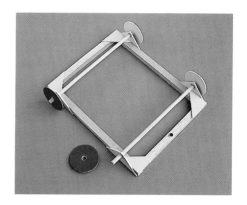

5 The dowel should turn easily. Glue a cardboard wheel to the ends of each dowel axle. Make sure each wheel is straight.

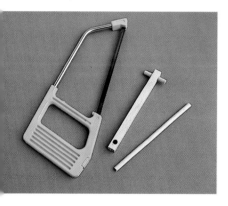

6 Drill two holes in the last piece of wood. Make one hole about .5 in. (1 cm) from the end, the other in the same place at the other end, but through the opposite sides of the wood. Tap a 1.5 in. (3 cm) piece of dowel through this hole to make a pulling handle.

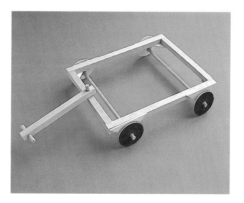

7 Tap the last 1.5 in. (3 cm) piece of dowel into the hole on the trailer frame. Put the handle on the trailer. You may need to use a needle file to make this hole in the handle bigger so the handle can move freely from side to side.

NOW TRY THIS

Glue a piece of cardboard onto the top of the chassis. Design and make a top for your trailer. It could be a flower seller's cart or perhaps a covered wagon.

Modern trucks are steered in the same way as the trailer on these pages. The front section of the truck can turn to the right or left. The back section follows in the direction it is pulled.

GRAVITY VEHICLE

YOU WILL NEED

- Lid of a shoe box

- Wooden dowel for axles, .25 in. (5 mm) in diameter: two pieces about .5 in. (2 cm) longer than the width of the box

- Wooden dowel, .25 in. (5 mm) in diameter: two pieces about 12 in. (30 cm) long, one piece 4 in. (10 cm) long

- Four circles of cardboard for wheels, about 2 in. (5 cm) in diameter, with center holes to match the dowel

- String or heavy thread

- Plastic modeling clay

- Glue

- Masking tape

- Hole punch

- Ruler

Before gasoline engines were invented, many different methods were tried to make vehicles move. Aside from steam engines, nothing worked as well as a horse. However, some people experimented with the energy of a falling weight.

1 Punch two pairs of holes in the sides of the box lid, 1 in. (2 cm) in from each end. Slide the dowel axles through the holes. Make sure they turn easily. Glue the wheels onto the ends of the axles.

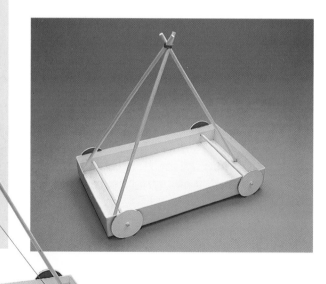

2 Glue the long pieces of dowel into the box lid, to form a pyramid. Two pieces should be at the front corners, and the third halfway along the back. Join them at the top with string and glue.

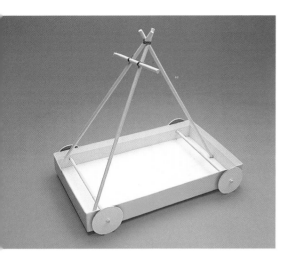

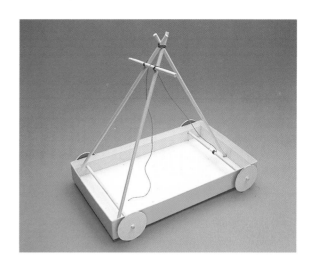

3 Tie the last piece of dowel across the front of the pyramid. Glue it as well. Attach it as near to the top as possible.

4 Cut a long piece of string. Stick one end to the rear axle and pass the other end over the dowel at the top of the pyramid.

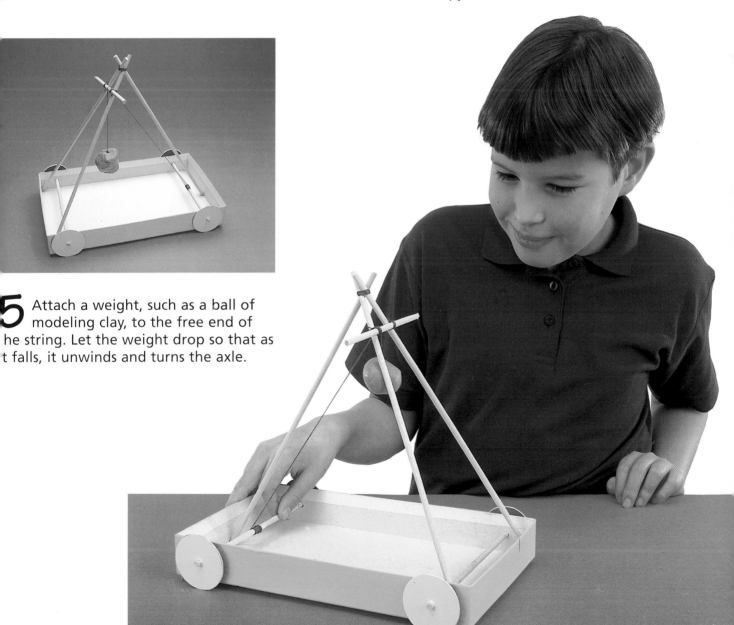

5 Attach a weight, such as a ball of modeling clay, to the free end of the string. Let the weight drop so that as it falls, it unwinds and turns the axle.

LAND YACHT

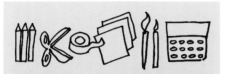

YOU WILL NEED

- Cardboard box, such as a shoe box
- Wood, about .5 in. (1 cm) square: two pieces about 6.5 in. (16 cm) longer than the length of the box
- Wooden dowel, .25 in. (5 mm) in diameter: two pieces 6 in. (14 cm) longer than the width of the box
- Wooden dowel, .25 in. (5 mm) in diameter: one piece for the mast (length depends on size of box)
- Four thread spools
- Four spring clothespins
- Four small pieces PVC tubing, about .25 in. (5 mm) in diameter and .25 in. (5 mm) long
- Tissue paper
- String or heavy thread
- Glue, masking tape, and scissors

All things need energy to make them move. Gasoline provides the energy for most cars and trucks. Other vehicles use electricity. It is even possible to use the energy of the wind to move some vehicles along.

1 Glue the two pieces of .5 in. (1 cm) square wood to the bottom of the box. The wood should stick out the same amount at either end of the box.

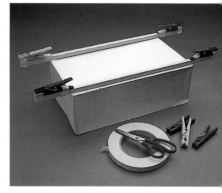

2 Attach the spring clothespins onto the ends of the wood, using masking tape. Clip the dowel axles into each pair of clothespins.

3 Slide a thread spool onto each end of the axles. Put the pieces of plastic tube on each end of the dowels to keep the spools on. The spools should run freely on the dowel axles.

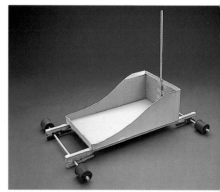

4 Cut the two long sides of the box to give it a streamlined shape. Attach the dowel mast to the inside of the box, in the center-front, using the masking tape.

Land yachting is a sport like sailing on water. A lightweight buggy is pushed along by the wind in the sail. A smooth land surface is needed, so the land yachts use flat, sandy beaches.

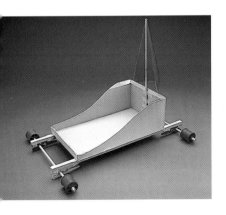

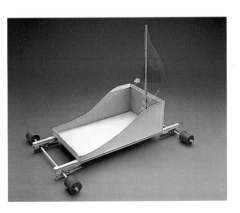

NOW TRY THIS

Design a different sail for your yacht. Try one with a boom, like a real sailboat or with a set of sails like old square-rigged sailing ships.

5 Cut a large triangle of tissue paper for the sail. Glue the top corner of the paper to the top of the mast, so that the sail hangs down in front of the mast.

6 Use masking tape to attach a length of thread to each bottom corner of the sail. Stick the other ends of the thread to the back edge of the box. The yacht is now ready to move.

ELECTRIC BUGGY

YOU WILL NEED

- Two empty plastic drink bottles

- Wood, about .25 in. (1 cm) square: two pieces about 12 to 16 in. (30 to 40 cm) long, depending on the size of the bottles

- Wooden dowel, about .25 in. (5 mm) diameter: two pieces 2.5 in. (6 cm) longer than the bottles

- Balsa wood: one piece about .25 in. (5 mm) thick, 3 in. (8 cm) wide and the same length as the dowel

- Four spring clothespins

- Small electric motor (1.5–4.5V)

- Battery (4.5V minimum)

- Single-core electric wire

- Rubber bands (various sizes)

- Masking tape

- Wire cutters & scissors

Some cars can be powered by electricity. They are clean and quiet. However, they are still at an early stage of development. In the future electric cars will work better, but at the moment they have little power, and their batteries need to be recharged every few miles (kilometers).

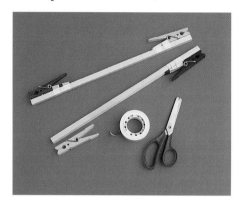

1 Using masking tape, attach a clothespin to each end of the .25-in. (1 cm) square wood.

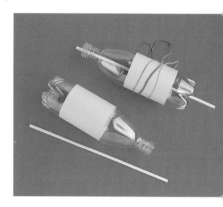

2 Make a hole in the bottom of each bottle. Put the dowel through the hole and out the top of each bottle. Put three or four different-sized rubber bands around one of the bottles.

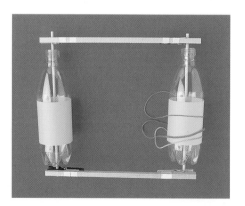

3 Clip each end of the dowel into the clothespins. The bottles should run freely but the axles should not move. If necessary, wrap some masking tape around the dowel to make it bigger.

4 Cut a .25 x .25 in. (1 x 1 cm) notch out of the edge of the balsa wood. Attach the motor firmly to the wood with masking tape. The spindle should be over the notch.

Electric cars do not make much noise and do not give off fumes. They are ideal for use in towns and cities. Many car manufacturers are working on electric cars, such as this one, for the future.

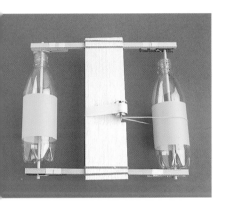

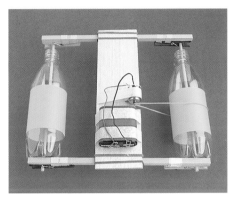

5 Use rubber bands to attach the balsa wood across the middle of the wood lengths, so that the motor faces the bottle that has the other rubber bands on it. Pull one of them over the spindle. Make sure it is not too tight.

6 Tape the battery to the wood next to the motor. Cut two wires and strip the ends. Attach them to the lugs at the back of the motor. Screw the wire into the battery terminal.

NOW TRY THIS

● Design and make a switch for the motor.
This needs to have two metal parts that can be put together and taken apart, such as two paper fasteners in a piece of cardboard. If you then make the wires long enough, you can walk alongside the buggy, holding the switch. This will make the buggy stop and start.

● Design and make a body to go over the buggy you have just made.

GLOSSARY

axle	A wood or metal rod on which a wheel turns.
boom	A pole on a ship. The sail is attached to it, and it has one end attached to the mast.
cable	A strong metal wire, used for electricity or to pull heavy loads.
chassis	The main frame of a vehicle, including axles and wheels. The body is attached onto it.
coach	Another name for a carriage, such as a horse-drawn or a train carriage.
diameter	The distance across the center of a circle, from one side to the other.
diesel	A type of fuel, used to drive engines.
fumes	Air or smoke that smells bad.
gravity	The pull of the earth that makes things fall to the ground when they are dropped.
jet	The push of air from an engine. This force can be used to drive a machine.
load	The weight raised or lowered by a machine or carried by a vehicle or animal.
passenger	A person who travels in a vehicle, boat, or aircraft.
pollution	Dirt in the air or on the land, such as smoke from cars or chemicals from factories.
pulley	A special wheel around which a rope is pulled to raise a weight or move an object.
recharged	Given more electricity. A recharged battery can continue working.
shaft	A straight wooden pole attached to the front of a cart.
spoke	A wooden bar or metal rod on a wheel. It is attached from the center to the rim.
springs	Curved or bent pieces of metal.
streamlined	Shaped specifically to move smoothly through air or water.
suspension	Springs and levers attached to the axles of a vehicle. These allow the body to move smoothly when the vehicle is moving over rough ground. This gives the passengers a more comfortable ride.
switch	A way of turning things such as lights or motors off and on by opening or closing the electric circuit.
template	A shape used to mark and cut out a number of the same shapes.
vehicle	Anything that carries people or freight.
yacht	A boat or vehicle that is pushed along by the wind.

BOOKS TO READ

Bendick, Jeanne. *Eureka! It's an Automobile.* Ridgefield, CT: The Millbrook Press, 1992.

Cars. Eyewitness Visual Dictionaries. New York: Dorling Kindersley, 1992.

Crickshank, Gordon. *Cars and How They Work.* See and Explore Library. New York: Dorling Kindersley, 1992.

Oxlade, Chris. *Cars.* 20th Century Inventions. Austin, TX: Raintree Steck-Vaughn, 1997.

Wilson, Anthony. *The Dorling Kindersley Visual Timeline of Transportation from the First Wheeled Chariots to Helicopters and Hovercrafts.* New York: Dorling Kindersley, 1995.

ADDITIONAL NOTES

Wobbly Wheels Making this simple design introduces children to the basic skills of measurement, cutting, and sawing. The axles must be properly in place, and the wood to be cut should be held securely in a vise.

Hovercraft This model is designed to show the scientific principles involved. It is very important to reduce the weight to the minimum and to see that no air can escape from under the tissue-paper "skirt."

Roman Chariot This simple model introduces children to new materials and to the idea of a fixed axle on which only the wheels themselves revolve. There is scope for further design.

Jet-Powered Car This model illustrates the importance of power-to-weight ratios. What power there is when air is expelled from a balloon is short-lived. The vehicle must be very light if it is to move at all, and there must be as little friction as possible between the wheels and axles.

Moon Buggy This model is based on a simple chassis. Plastic straws must be attached to the cardboard base with masking tape because airplane glue is not suitable for children of this age. Glue can be used to make the wheels and to stick anything to the top of the chassis.

Cable Car This model uses simple pulley wheels. Children of this age do not need to know the principles involved in using a block and tackle to lift a heavy weight. However, they can be introduced to the idea of a pulley as a method of facilitating movement.

Train Car and Tracks This model introduces children to the importance of special wheels for train tracks. There is plenty of scope for design work, both for the model and for the layout of the track.

Carriage with Suspension Although this model is made within a historical context, it introduces children to the modern idea of a chassis equipped with some form of spring. Modern suspensions are often a combination of levers and springs but can sometimes be made from rubber air cushions.

Trailer with Steering Handle Children will need to be shown how to use a small hand drill and can practice drilling holes in a spare piece of wood that should be fixed to the bench with a C-clamp.

Gravity Vehicle The idea for this type of vehicle was first considered by Hero in the second century B.C. He understood its limitations and so used it for self-moving scenery in his theaters. Used for this purpose, the vehicles had to move only very short distances.

Land Yacht Wind power has been used for land transportation since the early Chinese first put sails on barrows to help them carry heavy loads. A wind-powered vehicle was designed by Roberto Valturio in Italy during the 15th century, and a railroad car equipped with a sail was built in the 19th century.

Electric Buggy Electricity is a form of energy and can be used to drive a variety of vehicles. The clothespins can be used on many designs to hold axles and are convenient for changing wheel systems. Make sure that the rubber band is at the correct tension.

INDEX

Acknowledgments

The author and publishers wish to thank the following for their kind assistance with this book:
models Josie Kearns, Yasmin Mukhida, Charlotte Page, Tom Rigby and Ranga Silva. Also Gabriella
Casemore, Zul Mukhida, Philippa Smith, and Gus Ferguson.

For the use of their library photographs, grateful thanks are due to Eye Ubiquitous p8 (R Battersby), p13
(Darren Maybury), p16 (H. Rooney), p23 (David Gurr); James Davis Travel Photography, p5 top; Topham
Picturepoint p11, p15, p27, p29 (Citroen).
All other photographs belong to the Wayland Picture Library: p4 (Jimmy Holmes), p5 right (APM Studio),
p19 (Julia Waterlow), p20.